Wealth By Design

WAYS TO LOVE YOUR RETIREMENT™

Elisabeth M. Dawson

ISBN: 978-0-692-99356-9

"In the insurance industry, Elisabeth is one of the most qualified financial educators. Her honesty and integrity set her apart as someone you would benefit from working with. With this book, Elisabeth makes the often technical and complicated aspects of finance and insurance, simple and easy to understand. *Wealth By Design* is a wonderful, step-by-step 'how to guide' for people looking to live the life they've always imagined."

-Salvatore Petruzzella, CLU, ChFC, Industry Expert

"Elisabeth Dawson knows her stuff. She outlines the steps you need to make your money work for you. Elisabeth also lays out the discipline necessary to see the plan through and I can think of no one better to guide you through this process. This is a must-read for anyone who is ready to take control of their financial future!"

-Mike Steranka, Author, Retirement Specialist, and CEO of First Income Advisors

"Elisabeth Dawson is a premier planner in our industry. She is consistently at the top level, year in and year out. I would recommend this book to anyone looking to plan for retirement or anyone currently retired. Elisabeth has some great solutions for the 'retirement income epidemic' facing Americans today!"

-Brian Gengler, President of First Income Advisors

I dedicate this book
to understanding, knowledge and education;
to helping great people create an amazing life,
by design and not by casualties;
to consciously analyzing, strategizing, finding
solutions and supporting people in avoiding the
worry and emotional suffering that is commonly
attached to the psychology of money.

I recognize that money is the number one cause
for emotional distress in a person's life as an
individual, in their relationships, in their families,
in their friendships, in their businesses, in our
country and globally. When there is lack of
full clarity and understanding regarding the
relationship of money, anxiety and stress
overtake a life of quality and happiness.

That is why I dedicate this book to the passion
and caring effort of simplifying the complexity of
money and financial issues in all areas of life.
I take the coaching process seriously and deliver a
full view of money, great possibilities and precise
strategies. My work creates clarity and gives you
power over your finances, life and future.
In this society, it is a blessing when you have
respect for money and you value how you earn it,
how you manage it and how you multiply it.

The time to shape your future is now and
the first step always seems like the hardest.
It is my privilege and honor to support you
on your financial journey to freedom.

Table of Contents

Introduction

I am on a mission to help as many people as possible in this world achieve greatness in their financial lives which far exceeds their expectations. By focusing on education, guidance, and nurturing what's most important to every individual, I passionately believe in helping people to realize their ideal future.

Every day, millions of people wake up feeling stuck in the same routine and, unsurprisingly, continue to end up with largely the same results. Consider the well-known quote, often attributed to Einstein, which states the definition of insanity as, "Doing the same thing over and over again and expecting a different result." I am determined to stop the crippling effects which money anxieties commonly cause for so many people today; especially when the number one concern for individuals in retirement is running out of it! Are you one of those people? I know that you don't want to be.

Therefore, the conquering of my mission will require the help of each person reading this book to pass on its contents to everyone who deserves a better chance to get ahead. You work way too hard for your money every day to let it evaporate through the control of others. What are you doing to educate or prepare yourself to preserve your legacy or the legacy you have been so fortunate to receive? The answer to this defining question is all up to you.

As I say to many people, there is a professional for everything. Are you the financial professional in your life? Do you have an advisor who is asking you meaningful questions and performing above and beyond your expectations? Are they digging deeper and revealing to you what you need to know, or are they continuing to do the same things and expecting different results? I don't know about you but, as a financial professional, I am confident that settling for the definition of insanity will not help you achieve the life or retirement that you dream of living.

Life passes by quickly, and you deserve so much more than sleepless nights spent worrying about your retirement picture and your family's financial security. This is why I remain steadily dedicated to helping as many people as I can, in my lifetime. We all deserve a better future with financial independence and to be free from the burden caused by a fear of running out of money. I can help you to build and achieve your ideal retirement and thus, realize the life which you were meant to live!

-Elisabeth Dawson

Chapter 1

The Cost of Traditional Thinking

Every day, you make hundreds of seemingly ordinary decisions and carry out countless actions based on your life experiences and the principles which you have come to embrace. Some of these choices and actions may be subconscious, while others are highly deliberate. Regardless, it is important to appreciate the extent to which they continually impact your life.

Traditional core beliefs and values are paramount in shaping every aspect of your life and the principles you choose to practice. As a comprehensive advisor, I believe it is crucial to wholeheartedly embrace and respect the role such values play in each of my clients' lives and goals. However, I want you to consider something about yours for a moment.

Each day, you do business with financial institutions, banks, and government entities, impacting you and your lifestyle. These establishments all understand that you hold traditional core beliefs which form the bedrock of how you make every decision in your life today. Now, there is nothing wrong with these traditional thought processes. However, do you believe that the financial institutions, banks, government entities and especially the private businesses with which you conduct business, all within the sphere of your lifestyle, use your core beliefs and values to your advantage or their advantage?

Take a moment to reflect on what I am asking you here. Almost everyone tells me, when asked this question, that these entities use commonly held personal beliefs and values to their advantage, to increase profits, and against you, the individual. So, how does that make you feel? Horrible, right? Don't you want to know how to stop this from happening? Well, I am here to show you how.

These entities have been taking advantage of you for long enough. Now is the time to become educated so that you can be the one to take back control of your financial destiny, as opposed to continuing to give it away freely and unnecessarily. Are you ready to *do* something about it and take action? Are you ready to take massive action today? Or are you merely going to talk about it and allow things to continue down the same path?

As you travel through this book, please keep the following assertion in mind: It's not that your traditional core beliefs and values are not incredible principles. It is most important to understand that once you recognize that various societal entities are playing the game of life as your opponent, you need to educate yourself so you can win the game against them. Your leading enemies are taxes, fees, lost opportunity costs, wealth transfers, time, average rates of returns versus compounding rates of return and so much more.

So, what does this all mean and where do we start? It means you need a structured plan of attack that you could benefit from guidance in how to implement. To begin, let's explore a proven process I have successfully used to help countless clients. After all, there is no time like the present. So, let's start talking about this proven process; the first element of the *Wealth Acceleration Pathway*™.

Chapter 2

<u>Vision: Inventing Your Ideal Future</u>

Before I can begin to evaluate your financial picture and help you chart an effective course of action, it is crucial for me to understand what it is that you visualize for your ideal life and retirement. This is different for every individual and something only you can determine. I find the most difficult part of this process is realizing your ideal; imagining there are no obstacles standing between you and your desires for the future.

That's why during our initial meeting, together we explore your hopes, dreams and goals, as well as how they fit into the overall picture of the life and retirement you aspire to live. You will learn surprising strategies for making a meaningful transformation in your human, intellectual, financial and civic assets. Understanding what's possible empowers you to take the steps to turn your "wish list" into a list of accomplishments. Napoleon Hill, an American self-help author, said, "Whatever the mind of man can conceive and believe, it can achieve." That is indeed a crucial first step: awakening and training your mind to ruminate on your ideal life.

What does this all mean? Well, what do you want it to mean? This is *your* life and this is *your* wish list. This is someone asking you, perhaps for the first time in your life, what you truly want your life to be. No dream is too big and no request is too small. Your concerns are immensely valid and your current advisor, I promise you, is not dialed into what makes you tick. They want to know what extra two percent they can make for you (or honestly, themselves) in the marketplace. Meanwhile, your life dreams, hopes and values are often far from their number one concern.

This is where we break down, to the core, what you envision as your ideal reality. I honestly want to know what you work so hard for, every single minute of every single day. What have you chosen to make sacrifices for? What have you worked your entire life for? What do you want your legacy to be? What do you want your grandchildren to remember you for? More likely than not, it's your values and what you stood for in life.

I want to help you achieve the life you were meant to live. I am confident you can realize your ideal future, become what you were destined to become and can pass down a proud legacy to the ones you love. This visionary phase of our work together is about more than the American dream and bigger than each of us. Now is when we uncover *your* dream, so think big!

This is what the real vision meeting is all about: giving you the foundation and opportunity to invent your ideal future, without restrictions. So, have you begun to consider what you want your ideal future to look like?

Chapter 3

Wealth Acceleration Pathway

Over the course of moving through the *Wealth Acceleration Pathway*, you will benefit from my professional experience in a distinct way. Unlike many advisors, who are most concerned with how to invest your current assets to earn the highest commissions for themselves, my focus is uncovering the hidden costs of doing business with Wall Street and other financial institutions you interact with. Then, I develop a customized, well thought out plan that we agree on and you thoroughly understand. I emphasize establishing a comprehensive and coordinated approach which enables you to move confidently in the direction of your goals, dreams, desires, and making your "wish list" a "reality list."

You will learn about the key concepts, principles and strategies for accelerating your human, intellectual, financial, civic and financial wealth, starting right from wherever you are now. You'll receive clear advice with recommendations that will put you on the path to the future of your dreams.

You may have already acquired your wealth; now the challenge is to keep as much of it as possible, without others taking it from you unknowingly and unnecessarily. Or, perhaps you still have several years of work ahead of you to get to where you want to be. Regardless of where you currently are in your financial journey, it's important to be astute and remain diligent to reap the rewards you deserve and avoid being taken advantage of financially. Ask yourself: do you know every fee and cost associated with each of your accounts? Are they disclosed or non-disclosed? Are you prepared for how taxes will affect you each year? Upon the sale of a property? At the death of a loved one? Unfortunately, you can't avoid most common fiscal pitfalls simply by burying your head in the sand and hoping they won't adversely affect your bottom line.

What is a Lost Opportunity Cost?

Any dollar that you have lost due to a fee, have given away unnecessarily or unknowingly, and that you can no longer invest to receive earnings on over time, represents a lost opportunity cost. This cost must be measured and calculated over one's lifetime and this affects your net worth as a subtraction/loss, because you can never recover that dollar or its potential earnings.

As an example, consider some of the following common fees and expenses which the average American may incur over the course of a year:

Bank Fees: $12 a month ($144 per year)
ATM Fees: $3 non-bank withdrawal + $3 bank fee x 3 times a month ($216 per year)
Coffee Shop Habit: $9 a day x 4 days a week = $36 week ($468 per year)
Average Credit Card Fee: $150 per year
Average Credit Card Interest: $1,500 per year
Total Average Miscellaneous Costs: $194.50 per month, or $2,334 total per year

Now, most of this may not seem like much for the cost of doing business, but it sure adds up when you're not looking, or have fallen into a comfortable routine. If you could have invested that $2,334 per year, at an average interest rate of 6% over 20 years, that represents a lost opportunity cost of $91,009.02. This is a huge amount of wealth lost to these financial entities, which you freely paid to them. Why? Possibly out of convenience, or perhaps you ran out of time. It's easy to wrap your daily coffee run into your lifestyle and routine. You may want those credit card rewards and airline points but – at the end of the day – are those companies really giving you something for free for spending your money with them? Or, are they charging you so much more and taking advantage of you with distracting bonus miles and gift cards?

Let me give you some perspective. The financial entities you willingly give your money to are re-investing this money at a much higher rate of return than you are receiving. Think of common credit card companies and the interest rates they charge the average consumer. The Federal Reserve reported the APR across all credit card accounts averaged 13.08% for the third quarter of 2017.[1] However, the rates can vary drastically based on the type of card you have. In general, the more card benefits or the lower your credit score, the higher rate you will pay. I have seen rates as high as 29.97%. So, just take a minute to consider what the $2,334 per year from our example would grow to at a 29.97% interest rate over 20 years, or even 30 years. That potential loss of wealth over 20 years is more than $1.9 million. Meanwhile, over 30 years, it totals over $26 million. You can see why credit card companies and banks love you so much! They are creating wealth multiple times over from you.

You may say that you pay your cards off each month. However, let me remind you of all the fees I have mentioned; they all have different interest averages tied to them. The fact is, high fees have become pervasive in our society. Simply from the lost opportunity cost of $2,334 per year, illustrated in my example, you could potentially lose millions over the next 30 years of your lifetime. Now, I ask you: how much of that money do you want to recover? How much do you want back in your control?

My next question is: how much money do you
think I can find and help you recover? My
answer to you is: so much more than just
$2,334! On average, I find between $40,000 to
$60,000 per year, for my clients to recover and
re-allocate. How much wealth do you think they
can create with that?

If you stop to think about it, do you want to
continue to give away hundreds of thousands of
dollars in your overall lifetime? Or, do you want
that money in your control and available for
your future? After all, you earned it and you
deserve to have it. Do you still want to keep
giving your money away or do you want to start
recovering your wealth today?

Unfortunately, the average consumer often
wastes their money on fees such as these,
without much time for thought or reflection. I
regularly see even ten times as many fees as
this when analyzing a client's cash flow, so we
are just scratching the surface with the money I
am showing you here in this example.

My talent is to "find the money" for clients:
assets that financial institutions, banks, the

government and your lifestyle are taking away from you in excess. Then, together, we create a plan to recuperate the lost opportunity dollars I have found and help you recover your true wealth and put it to work for you! We accomplish this by establishing your own *Wealth Recovery Account*™, which we will take a closer look at in another chapter. But again, I ask you: do you want to continue to give $91,009.02 away over the next 20 years, if this example looks like you? I imagine your answer is no. So, when do you plan to do something about it? When will you take action to change your financial behavior and habits to recover your wealth? It does not have to be lost forever.

Chapter 4

Discovery and Review

As a crucial foundation within the process, I
take you through a structured, comprehensive
approach for understanding your current
human, intellectual, financial, and civic assets,
as well as your financial position, available
resources, untapped strengths and overlooked
or underused opportunities.

Are you investing in your number one
investment? First of all, what would you say *is*
your best investment? Most people believe, or
will tell me, that this is their home. Others
believe it's their retirement plan account(s).
Let's think about this for a minute. Is your
primary residence an asset or liability? Does it
produce an income or a cost for deferred
maintenance? How about your 401(k) or 403(b)?
Are your retirement plans the all-encompassing
answer to your retirement picture? They are
only a piece of the puzzle.

Think about what your best investment is...it is
YOU! Without you, your desires and visions for
the future do not exist; nothing matters. So,
why aren't you investing in yourself?

If you could invest in yourself, knowing that you
are the best investment in the world to invest
in, how much would you invest? $1? $5?
$10,000? $1,000,000? I sometimes hear, "As
much as I possibly can."

Now, the next question is this: if you invest in
yourself, how would you choose to spend the
money that you invest and, are you worth
it? Your children think so; your spouse thinks
so; your company thinks so.

Michael Jordan was the first individual who
invested in himself in the 1980's. He did so by
incorporating himself. Everyone knows who he
is; especially his family, who are likely to benefit
from his immense estate. He has a net worth of
$1.31 billion and has been investing in himself
for a long time, asking for as much as he
could. However, you do not have to be a
professional athlete to invest in yourself.

How does this fit into what am I talking about? It has to do with finding out what your real economic value is, based on your level of income and your net worth. This can be done by determining your earning capacity over your working years, or using your total net worth, and having an insurance company insure your human economic value for that amount in permanent insurance. Then, you can follow an established plan for saving real dollars to invest in yourself for the power and control to be able to spend and protect your human economic value over your lifetime.

The first question I ask people at this stage is: if you could spend down the death benefit of your well designed permanent life insurance policy over your lifetime, how much economic value, or death benefit, would you like to have? Some of it? All of it? Or none of it?

The second question I ask is: if you could spend this benefit, tax-free, over your lifetime would that influence your decision even more? Now, it is important to note that the distribution design you decide on during this phase determines the ability of funds to be paid out tax-free and must be followed without cancellation of the contract. Otherwise, tax consequences may occur. This step of the process can be complicated and is one of the many reasons why I am here to help.

In discussing insurance, please make no mistake; this is not about simply having a term insurance policy until it gets too expensive, then letting it expire to end the contract. That is a true loss of wealth. If you had $2,000,000 in the stock market one day and the stock market had a horrible crash the next day, and your account went to $0, would that be a bad day? Of course it would. There is no difference when a $2,000,000 life insurance asset leaves your life. Don't let this happen to you.

Term insurance actually equates to being the largest lost opportunity cost for a family. Even so, term policies are frequently purchased and recommended over permanent policies because the insurance company makes the highest profit on selling term insurance. Meanwhile, the likelihood of you dying before age 65 is less than 2%.[2] Why would you want to pay tens of thousands of dollars in premiums to a policy which your heirs will most likely never see a benefit from? What benefit will that expired term policy provide when you need it the most: when you actually die? Ben Feldman, American businessman and author said, "The best investment in the world is the one that pays the most when you need it the most, and that's life insurance." However, having the right kind of life insurance is just as important as having any at all.

Term insurance is death insurance and no one I have met wants to die young; they want to live long, healthy lives. We always plan for clients to live to age 100 and beyond, which you simply can't do with term insurance. Since it merely acts as a Band-Aid to temporarily fill a gap, the best use of term insurance would be to help you obtain more permanent insurance based on your current insurability. This can be helpful by capitalizing on your present good health because you can be insured and protected today until you obtain permanent insurance, without again having to prove you are healthy a few years down the road.

Now, let me be clear: if you have to have term insurance at younger ages to afford to cover your family, that's still a good decision. However, it is widely known in the finance community that a relatively small percentage of all term insurance ever actually pays out. Therefore, the question you need to keep in mind is: where would you like to put your money for the long haul? A sure thing or a maybe?

Let's look at an example of human economic value using fictitious clients, Mr. and Mrs. Wealth By Design.

Mr. Wealth By Design is currently 55 years of age, with a target retirement age of 67 (his age of full retirement for Social Security). Therefore, he expects to have another 12 working years at his annual salary of $175,000.

$175,000 Annual Earnings
x 12 Years
$2,100,000 Human Economic Value

So, Mr. Wealth By Design's human economic value is $2,100,000. To calculate how long this benefit will take care of his spouse and other heirs in the event of his passing, we simply divide the $2,100,000 by $175,000 of annual income, to estimate 12 years.

As you can see, it's not necessarily about making someone rich when you die; it's about providing the economic income they will need to ensure that they have the means to take care of themselves when the event occurs. Using this strategy simply replaces the asset which doesn't tangibly exist and fills that gap. If there are additional assets you have accumulated which will provide guaranteed income for the rest of your life, then you can decrease your human economic valuation, or what I call your *asset protection calculation*. However, I have never met anyone who wants to have a drastically lower income when a spouse respectfully exits this life – or anytime for that matter. That is why I show you how to plan for "the gap," or the revenue loss which can often result from a person passing away. I can help to determine and establish the assets which need to perform and provide for the surviving spouse, regardless of who predeceases whom. This *Asset Protection Calculation* is even more crucial if there are children or elder family members who are dependent upon the income provider(s) as well.

As they say, we are only guaranteed two things in life: death and taxes. Not exactly in that order, but possibly. Someone also once told me, "We will not get out of here alive." It may sound like I'm joking here, but it's the truth. Every day is immensely precious and, as I write this, a very dear friend just lost her father this evening. Unfortunately, it often takes a tragedy or catastrophic event to remind us just how fragile life can be.

So, going back to the example, let's make this conversation a bit more fun and intriguing for Mr. and Mrs. Wealth By Design.

"Mr. and Mrs. Wealth By Design, if you could (figuratively) spend the death benefit of your life insurance contract while you are alive, how much life insurance would you like to have?"

What I usually hear at that point is, "How can you do this?"

Then I ask the next question, "Well, if you could (figuratively) spend the death benefit of your life insurance contract while you are alive, *tax-free*, how much would you like to have?"

People will tell me, "As much as I can get!"

That is what I show my clients how to do. I can show you, first, how to invest in yourself as your best investment and, secondly, how to spend down your best investment as a tool for a tax-free cash flow strategy.

First and foremost, you have to qualify. This is important because not everyone can. However, if *you* can't specifically, your spouse, your children or even your grandchildren possibly can. You can always be the owner of those contracts and still reap the benefits of what we are talking about here.

I meet with individuals all the time who do not need life insurance. However, when I show them what an incredible tool permanent, well designed whole life insurance can be for those who qualify, people choose to employ it within their portfolio.

The biggest obstacle standing in many peoples' way is comfortably affording the premium to contribute to their personally designed plan. This is where I can assist as well. Nearly everyone wants life insurance; they just don't want to sacrifice their lifestyle to pay for it. That is why I never compromise a client's lifestyle to pay for insurance premiums. I take it from everyone else who is trying to take it away from you. You deserve this wealth, not anyone else.

Find Me the Money

People tell me all the time that they have no money. I always assure them that it's not their problem, it's mine. This is what I do; this is my talent; I help people *find the money*! This is one of the reasons my approach is so well received and in such demand. If you don't believe me, challenge me. I'll find money you don't think you have.

I find tens of thousands, if not hundreds of thousands, of dollars annually for people who are serious about creating wealth. Hard-earned money, in clients' lives, that they are losing each and every year to financial institutions, banks, the government and the companies they choose to do business with over the course of their daily life. No one is forced to do this, but many people choose to do so voluntarily, simply out of convenience or because they do not know of a better way. I can show you how to change this in your life and you can reap the massive rewards. But first, you have to ask yourself if you are serious. Do you really want to change? Do you really want to learn? Are you coachable? Are you willing to change the way you do the things in your life to welcome much better results? If you are, then you can attain far superior outcomes. Call me, and get ready! This is work, but there is no better use of your time and effort. I am ready and waiting to help you.

That is my talent. I help clients to find money in their current financial situation that is being lost to wealth transfers, fees, lost opportunity costs, and more. On average, with a client/couple earning in the neighborhood of

$175,000 worth of income, I will find more than $45-$50,000 per year that is going to such areas. I show my clients how to recover these losses and put them into their *Wealth Recovery Account*, as we will discuss in further detail in the next chapter.

Each person I work with is their number one and most important asset. With the work and heavy lifting on my part and a little discipline on my clients' part, together we take the necessary steps for self-investment. The best part of this phase of my work with clients is the potential to generate tax-free benefits if positioned correctly within the current estate tax laws.

There are two common notions I have found to be true for practically everyone: that people never like to lose money and they never like to pay more than their fair share of taxes. After all, people work so hard for their money, their families, the lifetime of their estates, everything they believe in, and no one wants to see it wasted away. Once again, I am talking about you, not a product. This is about investing in you. Don't let taxes or the government take advantage of what is yours.

Chapter 5

Your Wealth Recovery Account

As one of the first steps towards implementing your plan and obtaining financial success, I will help you to initiate a *Wealth Recovery Account.*

What Is It?

Simply stated, your *Wealth Recovery Account* (WRA) is a separate checking account that acts as a temporary holding tank for money. It is a wealth building recovery strategy to stimulate your robust financial health and structure. This is where recovered costs, such as term insurance premiums, interest payments and dividends, will be recaptured. It is also the account from which payments for the new wealth-accumulating programs will be made (i.e., permanent life insurance, municipal bonds, real estate). The account should be established and labeled properly, as your WRA.

It is important to note that the "found money" classes we identify are recognized through cash flow analysis work, which I will comprehensively complete *with* you. This is how I educate you on overpaying costs and show you how to recover them. Then I show you how to re-direct this "found money" into your *Wealth Recovery Account.* When was the last time anyone wanted to help you find money vs. charging you money for everything?

What Your Wealth Recovery Account Is *NOT*

It is not your household account for daily cash flow transactions. It is not for expenses such as auto or homeowners' insurance, mortgage payments, credit card payments, etc. It is not another "lifestyle" account.

What Is the Purpose of Your Wealth Recovery Account?

Its primary purpose is to implement and track the financial moves previously agreed upon during the personal financial engineering process. It will automatically keep money circulating throughout your financial system, thereby maximizing wealth and benefits. This is accomplished due to the following:

1. All inputs to investments are handled through your WRA.

2. The transfer of money from your protection, savings and growth accounts is also passed to your WRA. Similarly, the movement of dollars from one account to another within the same component is also passed through this account. This process is called "coordination and integration." This may include adding "new money" to the WRA through regularly scheduled contributions to the model.

The secondary purpose of the WRA is to serve as an exclusive financial register for review purposes. A permanent record of all financial transactions is established for tracking the wealth recovery process. It is a log of transactions providing documentation for present and future tax considerations, such as cost basis and investment expenses.

What Are the Wealth Recovery Account Benefits?

The WRA produces many benefits that include the following:

1. Complete segregation of funds. Dollars for savings and investment are not commingled with vacation funds, emergency dollars or spending money.
2. A monthly statement documenting all transactions.
3. A financial case history carried forward from year to year.
4. Repositioning of assets is recorded through the source of the deposit and ultimate disposition of that deposit.
5. It serves as a clearinghouse for transactions. Your wealth is not misappropriated or spent unknowingly.
6. It provides accountability for reviews, which is often missing in traditional financial planning.

How to Set Up Your Wealth Recovery Account

What are the Requirements?

1. This account must be a checking account (either interest-bearing or non-interest-bearing) with the capability for direct deposits and automatic drafts. Please note that most money market accounts will not work.

2. This is your special "business" account, so you may wish to request that your checkbook reflect a business format with three checks per page and descriptive stubs beside each check. However, this is not mandatory.

3. You should use a bank where you do not currently hold accounts.

4. Talk to your bank's customer service representative to determine the option that will best suit these requirements.

What is Deposited into Your Wealth Recovery
Account?

_____ Interest formerly compounded on any
investments

_____ Dividends formerly reinvested

_____ Short term capital gains formerly
reinvested

_____ Long term gains formerly reinvested

_____ Recovered tax savings

_____ Savings from lower deductibles

_____ Recovered term premiums

_____ New money created by bonuses and
additional income

_____ New rents which can be saved

_____ Savings from refinanced debt

_____ Tax refunds

_____ Savings from tax (W-2) adjustments

_____ Dollars already allocated for life
insurance premiums

_____ Investment "pay downs"

What Will Be Drafted/Paid from Your Wealth Recovery Account?

_____ Life insurance premiums

_____ Disability insurance premiums

_____ Investment opportunities

     _____ Stocks

     _____ Bonds

     _____ Mutual Funds

     _____ Real Estate

     _____ Collectibles

_____ Life Insurance policy loan repayments

Establishing and maintaining a *Wealth Recovery Account* is a significant first step in getting you started on the path to improving your financial development.

Chapter 6

Present Plan: Your Current Financial Snapshot

After gaining an in-depth understanding of your current situation, I create a one-page analysis to evaluate where you are in relation to your goals; the products, tools and strategies you have; and a list of action items for you to complete. I have found this to be productive because it helps to convert a seemingly overwhelming and abstract idea into a tangible evaluation and effective action plan for clients. To put it simply, I strive to make complicated situations straightforward and help my clients to understand so that it is easier to embrace and implement the process.

I have reviewed financial plans for thousands of real people and worked with various advisors all over the country and the one aspect that I continuously see is that every single individual, or couple, is so incredibly focused on accumulation. Not that there is anything wrong with accumulation; obviously, it is a key component in generating wealth. The problem lies in becoming so focused on accumulation that it ends up consuming all of your time and energy. As a result, you end up doggedly pursuing the idea of wealth and trying to make all the money you can over your lifetime, without stopping to consider what it's all for.

Without considering your unique underlying purpose and true driving force, how do you even know in what direction you are really moving? Is all of your work for you, or for a dream that might just not happen? The financial services industry has been so hyper-focused on average rates of return, accumulation, and an, "I can beat this, I can beat that," mentality, that everyone is missing what is important: you and your ideal future.

Without stopping to evaluate your progress and periodically reassess your pathway, how likely do you think it is that you will reach your intended goals? Are you building wealth for you to be able to enjoy in your life? To pass down to your children and grandchildren? Or are you building your wealth up every day, only to spend it down through the government? Unfortunately, without a well thought out and executable action plan in place, I regularly see the latter happening most often. People have more wealth being exposed to taxes than ever before, simply due to poor planning. In fact, solid planning takes on even greater importance as assets accumulate since there is more at risk to lose. Wealth creation is a wonderful thing; however, when you are paying taxes, month after month and year after year, over the course of your life and then again upon your death, it's not a favorable scenario.

Consider the following table, which outlines the cost of probate fees incurred by an estate when a living trust or will has not been established. Even if you don't think your estate is that large, you still need to plan. After all, if you don't proactively take control, you are likely to face staggering fees.

PROBATE ADMINISTRATION

CALIFORNIA STATUTORY COMPENSATION
for Attorney & Executor in a Probate Administration
Based on Fair Market Value of Decedent's Property

Formula: 4% of the first $100,000; 3% of the next $100,000, 2% of the next $800,000; 1% of the next $9,000,000; 0.5% of the next $15,000,000

FMV of Property	Attorney Fees	Executor Fees	Total Fees
$100,000	$4,000	$4,000	$8,000
$125,000	$ 4,750	$4,750	$9,500
$150,000	$5,500	$5,500	$11,000
$175,000	$6,250	$6,250	$12,500
$200,000	$7,000	$7,000	$14,000
$300,000	$9,000	$9,000	$18,000
$400,000	$11,000	$11,000	$22,000
$500,000	$13,000	$13,000	$ 26,000
$700,000	$17,000	$17,000	$34,000
$900,000	$21,000	$21,000	$42,000
$1,000,000	$23,000	$23,000	$46,000
$1,250,000	$25,500	$25,500	$51,000
$1,500,000	$28,000	$28,000	$56,000
$2,000,000	$33,000	$33,000	$66,000
$3,000,000	$43,000	$43,000	$86,000
$4,000,000	$53,000	$53,000	$106,000
$5,000,000	$63,000	$63,000	$126,000
$10,000,000	$113,000	$ 113,000	$226,000

*Probate table courtesy of Rodriguez Law Offices, San Diego, CA. www.RodriguezLawOffices.com

It's time to become educated about your options. As Bob MacDonald, the founder of LifeUSA Insurance and retired CEO of Allianz, North America states, "The primary reason people stop learning is the assumption they know all they need to know." In today's busy world, I think we can all agree that there just isn't enough time to know everything as in depth as we might wish we could. As a result, we may often find ourselves assuming we know enough. However, to consider the effects that knowledge gaps can have on your financial life, whether you are aware of them or not, is rather alarming. I can help you discover what you didn't even know you were missing, in addition to how it is affecting your overall financial state. Not only that, but most important, we can also show you how to proceed in a more prudent direction using your new knowledge to effectively restructure your financial future.

Chapter 7

Success Formula

The best financial plan in the world will never work if it isn't appropriately executed. I work tirelessly to ensure that does not happen to my clients. While I welcome and encourage questions throughout the entire process, this meeting is specifically prepared to ensure your understanding of necessary financial principles and the recommended "success formula" for your financial and civic assets. Some of these key areas include wealth transfers, recovering lost opportunity costs, and getting one dollar to do the work of many. I also help you discover hidden assets (both monetary and other assets) as we find and plug "money leaks" together.

If there is ever anything you don't understand within all that we discuss, I always want to slow it down and encourage you to ask the questions that will help you to make sense of it all. I never want to be the advisor just telling you how it goes, with you following the magic formula and expecting it all to work out. I want you working right alongside me, as a partnership, helping the decision-making process occur all along the way. This is a team effort and not only is your success my success, but implementing your legacy is my greatest achievement.

My highest accomplishment is seeing your family and future generations respecting the wealth you have created over all the years that you have worked so hard. Statistics show when significant wealth passes down from one generation to the next, it is usually completely gone by the third generation. In fact, according to a 2013 study from researchers at the Williams Group wealth consultancy, featured in the Wall Street Journal, nearly 70% of family money disappeared after the second generation and 90% was gone after the third generation.[3] That is a depressing figure, especially since much of the wealth may be squandered rather than actually benefiting the recipients. I care about the future wellbeing of your successors and if you don't want this to happen, I will work to prevent it. By educating and counseling each generation of the family to respect the value of what you have worked so hard for, the third and fourth generations will be just as driven as you to preserve and protect your legacy going forward.

Of course, first and foremost, I want to see you fully enjoy the fruits of your labor by spending your hard-earned wealth on whatever it is that you desire. After all, you deserve to take pleasure in the reward for all of your years of hard work and dedication. We can make that happen. How? By working just as hard on the distribution phase of your assets as you do on the accumulation of your assets.

Chapter 8

Income Planning and Pension Income

With so much industry focus on the accumulation of wealth, many people fail to realize that the distribution phase can be the most complicated phase of your lifetime. Retirees are no longer working and now it's up to their assets to produce the income needed to support their lengthy retirement ahead.

Suppose you are fortunate enough to amass $1 million within your retirement accounts over your working years. While saving $1 million for retirement may sound like a lot, market statistics today estimate that amount could last less than 17 years in retirement, depending upon your state of residence.[4] As a result, more people are pressured with the lasting burden of continuing to generate income for the rest of their life in retirement.

The Social Security Administration estimates about one of every four 65-year-olds today will live past age 90, with one of every 10 living beyond age 95.[5] As I write this, I am on a plane traveling to New York to celebrate my Grandmother's 100th Birthday. She never dreamed that she would live to age 100 and she is celebrating over 45 years in retirement. Could that be you one day, too?

I recently read an article which states that the average widow in the United States is age 59. This means they could live another 30 or more years in retirement. The article also stated that when couples are planning their financial lives, in the majority of relationships, the financial decisions are largely made by the husband. Only 3% of married women drive the financial conversations for their household.[6] This is drastic and needs more attention. It is my passion to make sure that both spouses, both partners, and all parties involved, know what is going on in their financial lives. In every decision, all parties should be on board. This approach is crucial due to the cause and effect of every financial decision. Not only are parties' immediate lives affected but, more importantly, there are lasting repercussions once one person passes away.

You have to ask yourself, do your assets have the spending power to pay your average income in retirement for the next 26 to 45 years, or more? To be realistic, the traditional financial planning methods of those who have planned for a 20-year retirement have resulted in a huge population who have planned for failure. Why? People are living far longer than they ever dreamed of, due to a combination of factors including longer life expectancy rates, advanced medicine and improved health technology, as well as many people simply taking better overall care of themselves than in the past.

Without question, the number one concern people retiring express to me, is not having enough money to retire or the fear of running out of money in retirement. Not only is this a central concern for many individuals today, but it's also one of the most commonly held uncertainties across the aging population. Most people are correct and their fears are well-founded. So how do you alleviate this fear?

Definitely not by being professional procrastinators, which is unfortunately what happens in many cases since people often envision comprehensive retirement planning as an overwhelming and insurmountable task.

Start planning for your retirement in advance; you owe it to yourself. Not a few weeks or months in advance, but years in advance. When you retire, you want to *stay* retired – and without compromising your quality of life. Feeling secure and being able to pursue your true desires in retirement is your hard-earned reward and I believe in helping you to accomplish all that you've envisioned your retirement to be.

We are living in an era where you could be spending more in retirement than during the years that you worked, but do your accumulated assets have what it takes to make this happen? Let's take this even a step further. What if you could protect your assets in retirement and turn them into a personal pension that would pay you a guaranteed income stream for the rest of your life? Would you do it? Of course you would.

As a society, we face a longevity problem ahead of us and we, as individuals, need to make sure that our income will sustain us no matter what, even as traditional pensions in the US continue to vanish. In fact, the majority of privately owned companies today no longer offer pension options to their employees. While this is partially due to the economic climate in recent years, there has also been a substantial cultural shift with regard to the workplace. Previous generations saw many individuals working for one employer throughout the majority of their careers. In turn, employees were guaranteed a comfortable pension upon their retirement as a reward for their decades of service. Such pensions were often generous and continued to pay out until the passing of the former employee. However, in more recent years, there has been a dramatic shift across the country as many people today may continue to "job hop" throughout the entirety of their working years. A considerable consequence of this change is the loss of traditional pension plans and the impact it will have on millions of future retirees.

In addition to many companies electing to no longer offer pension options to their employees, there is also a growing pattern of pension plans that face bankruptcy due to the inability to sustain assured payouts to workers who have earned them. While frightening to imagine, too many working individuals today may not yet grasp the resulting burden poised to land squarely on their shoulders, appointing them as the sole provider of their own financial security throughout their retirement years.

It is for this reason, once again, that the majority of people approaching retirement are beginning to question whether they will actually be able to stop working, and the fear of running out of money is mounting. However, while the momentum behind the loss of traditional pension plans within our society may be unavoidable, the resulting anxiety and excessive personal burden do not have to take control in its wake.

Let's consider a case study which explores the powerful impact which prudent income planning can have on your overall retirement picture.

Case Study

An average couple, getting ready to retire, were introduced to me through existing clients of mine. In this case, the couple wanted to get a second opinion from me to see if their current retirement plan was as strong as they believed it would be. So, I happily took a look at what they wanted me to review.

Both the husband and wife were age 65 and ready to retire. He worked for a company that would pay him a pension of $60,000 per year, and upon retirement he could receive Social Security payments of $2,400 per month, for a total of $28,000 per year. Or, if he waited to collect Social Security until his full retirement age of 66.4, he would receive $2,600 per month, or $31,200 per year. He was determined to retire as soon as possible so I ran the projections for him to begin taking Social Security at age 65.

His wife also had a small pension from working for a company for many years, although it was not as much as her husbands. It was going to pay her about $9,000 per year. She was also eligible for Social Security at age 65 for a reduced benefit of $1,100 per month, or $13,200 per year. She knew that she would not have a large pension when she retired, and had saved over $250,000 in a 401(k) throughout her working years. So, here is what their existing plan looked like.

$60,000 – Husband's Pension
$28,000 – Husband's Social Security
$9,000 – Wife's Pension
$13,200 – Wife's Social Security
$110,200 – Total Annual Income

Their annual income, while both were working, was in the neighborhood of $145,000. Therefore, they knew they would be taking a pay cut of about $35,000 when they retired, which they both felt they could handle. However, it became clear that they failed to take several other factors into consideration when I began asking some very important questions.

Respectfully, my role requires that I ask the difficult questions. Questions that, under most circumstances, people may not want to even think about, much less answer or discuss. However, these questions need to be addressed to foster prudent planning. For example:

1. How comfortable does it feel to live off of $35,000 less in income per year?

If you don't like that idea, you probably won't like my next question either.

2. What happens to your household income if one spouse passes away at age 70? Age 75? Age 80? What if the other spouse passes away first?

For this couple, with their existing plan, here is what her survivorship income would look like if he passed away.

$30,000 – Husband's Pension (Drops by ½)
$28,000 – Keep Husband's Social Security
$9,000 – Wife's Pension
$0 – Lose Wife's Social Security
$67,000 – Total Annual Income

Their income just dropped by $43,200 per year for her. That's a 39.2% loss of income per year, regardless of how the market or economy are performing. Do you think most people even think about this before it happens to them?

From what I know to be true for couples out there today, most have household bills that are usually based on the total a family is earning, not just what half of the income coming in can afford to pay. Not everyone's house is paid off, and many people may continue to carry mortgage debt well into their retirement years, as well as property taxes and insurance costs.

There are so many factors in our lives which are beyond our control that it is crucial to take command of what you can. You want to be equipped to face as many possibilities and unknowns in your future as you can while continuing to live your best life today.

If a long-term care event occurs in this couple's future, could it affect their life savings and assets? Absolutely. If you can imagine yourself as the survivor here; could you live on an annual pay cut of about $78,000 less than what you were used to living on while you were working? I haven't met anyone who thought they could.

This is what's called an income or asset gap: an individual doesn't have enough assets to fill the gap in income they lose in the event the main income provider dies before the other spouse. You may be wondering, can this be avoided? Yes! Not only can this be avoided, but doing so is part of my main focus, right from the start, when I have the privilege to be a part of the retirement planning process with clients and their families. I don't want you to be faced with a large asset gap or suffer from that kind of predicament, and I know that you don't either. So please, let me show you how to find solutions to redirect and correct this dire problem.

Now, lately the market has been doing well, but what if there is another significant correction, as occurred in 2000, 2001, 2002 "the dot.com era" or the major correction of 2008? Could that happen again? Maybe it will, maybe it won't, but it is certainly possible.

If you recall, the wife had a 401(k) worth $250,000 as she reached retirement. However, the wife was a bit more conservative and wanted to protect the hard-earned money which she had saved in her 401(k). She wanted to protect it from loss in the event there was a market correction, but she also wanted to take advantage of the market going up: the best of both worlds. At the same time, she needed to establish an income stream to supplement her existing pension. Essentially, she needed to create her own personal pension out of this money and have a guaranteed income source throughout retirement, regardless of market fluctuation.

To accomplish her goals, she allocated this portion of her money to a fixed indexed annuity offering all the above-mentioned possibilities. In addition, in her situation, she was unrestricted and enjoyed the flexibility of deferring withdrawals until she was ready to take income from her account. How tremendous is that? So, if she wanted to take income immediately, she could have taken $11,700 per year, as a guaranteed amount of income for the rest of her life. However, she didn't need income immediately so I could position her to have her principal grow until about age 70 and begin to take the income at that time. Thus, if her $250,000 grew at an average amount of 6% per year, she would then have $334,556 and the guaranteed income for life would be an estimated payment of $16,728 per year. That is $5,028 more per year, for as long as she lives, and equivalent to 43% more income just five years later. The considerable increase caused by deferring her income payments can help to fill some of the gap that she will one-day face.

One crucial fact to point out here is that not all annuities are the same. Within the strategy that we have spoken about here, the client never gave up control of her money to the financial institution. If she ever needed a distribution from the account, she could take it. It would affect her annual income distribution, but she never loses control of her asset because she never has to annuitize her account. That loss of control, and being forced to annuitize an account in order to receive payments is what gave previous annuities a bad name in years past. However, newer annuity products offer more options than ever before, without the owner ever having to separate themselves from the asset once they begin taking income. This means that any remaining account balance left upon their passing goes to their beneficiaries, heirs and/or estate; it never stays with the insurance company.

Now, look at what her survivorship income would be if her husband respectfully passes away at age 70.

$30,000 – Husband's Pension (Drops by ½)
$28,000 – Keep Husband's Social Security
$9,000 – Wife's Pension
$0 – Lose Wife's Social Security
$16,728 – Wife's Protected 401(k)
$83,728 – Total Annual Income

Is that a little better than $67,000? Absolutely.

Not everything is fixed yet, but their situation has improved. Now let's use the *Asset Protection Calculation* to determine what is still missing. First, we find the difference between their total combined annual income and her new estimated survivorship income to determine the remaining annual income shortfall.

$110,200 Income, While Both Living
- $83,728 Improved Income
$26,472 Deficit per Year

Next, we take the $26,472 per year and multiply it by their combined life expectancy of age 91, since there is a 50% chance one of them will reach age 91. This calculation illustrates the asset gap.

$26,472 Deficit
x 26 Years
$688,272 Asset Gap

This is the value needed to fill the asset gap in the event that he dies before her and she lives to age 91.

So, what does this all mean? Well, looking at it in another way, an asset in the amount of $688,272 divided over 26 years would give her $26,472 per year to make her survivorship income whole. Since they do not currently have such an asset, it needs to be created. This would enable her to continue to live comfortably and avoid creating a financial burden for her, as the person left behind. Ultimately, this is successfully achieving what they both worked so hard for throughout their lives together.

One way they can accomplish this goal is by using discounted dollars to purchase a well-designed, permanent life insurance policy for the calculated amount. This will cover the asset protection gap and grant her a sense of financial security in the event of his passing. In this case, the premiums for the life insurance were found through a cash flow analysis. This is a thorough examination which I specialize in doing for my clients when they engage in the process through their Found Money Report. Most significantly, this does not affect their lifestyle or additional spending.

With this solution implemented, the couple's final chosen scenario looked like this, in the event of the husband passing prior to the wife.

$30,000 – Husband's Pension (Drops by ½)
$28,000 – Keep Husband's Social Security
$9,000 – Wife's Pension
$0 – Lose Wife's Social Security
$16,728 – Wife's Protected 401(k)
$26,472 – Husband's Life Ins. Proceeds
Create this Income Each Year
$110,200 – Total Annual Income

No matter what, they will always have the same income, regardless of their ages, plus any additional cost of living adjustments for Social Security increases. Wouldn't you like to have that financial security in your life?

It's clear to see the dramatic effect the use of a comprehensive illustration such as an Income for Life Report can have in creating a thorough financial plan. Not only does it enable you to confidently make critical decisions which can influence the rest of your life, but it makes the process of doing so straightforward and minimizes anxiety since you can clearly and immediately see their impact.

Chapter 9

Wealth Acceleration Strategies

To effectively determine an appropriate course of action, you must first have a strong and complete understanding of your present financial position. I give you a clear numerical strategy "x-ray" of your current economic environment: this is the road you're heading down. Together, we'll identify both real and potential problems. This process will show you how to make better financial decisions by encouraging an examination of existing resources.

I ask this question to every client that I meet with: "How well do you understand Wall Street?" Believe me, few will claim that they fully understand. I recently had someone tell me, "We have a lot of money that is not doing a lot." He had well over a million dollars in the market that he had been managing himself for the past 20 years. His balance was modestly moving along. I shared with him the historical performance of the market, comparing it against his investment and performance for that same time period. While it showed the market earning an average of 9.99%, he only net a .5% rate of return over that period of time, due to his fees and expenses in the marketplace. His lower average had nothing to do with any greater market risk or volatility; it was what he was left with after expenses.

How many of you reading this book right now have found yourself scratching your head, feeling like there's something wrong with your portfolio, without being able to identify exactly what it is? You just can't seem to get ahead, and even after so many years of the market making money, you still don't feel that you are benefiting from its gain. Or, perhaps not as much as you think you should be. There is always a reason for these questions and observations.

The reality is that fees are eating people alive! To have any hope of getting ahead, you have to demand that your assets work harder for you, in environments where they can make more money with the least amount of fees, costs, and expenses. We work with our clients to achieve this on a daily basis. Now, you can't realistically expect to invest your full portfolio and have your capital growing yet protected, all while incurring absolutely no cost. However, you *can* eliminate your risk by shifting it all to businesses that will better benefit you; this will help your assets perform better, eliminate your undue risk, and avoid financial pitfalls along the way. In doing so, you can watch your portfolio far exceed your expectations, and even surpass what you may have imagined as possible for your assets.

We have been operating within such inconsistent financial environments for so long. Isn't it time to take control and demand some consistency to the outcomes of your immediate, future and retirement savings?

Chapter 10

Action Blueprint

As you may expect, the precise path to success and the essential steps to achieving financial security vary with every individual and their unique circumstances. The *Action Blueprint* is a visual model that shows you a set of custom strategies for achieving wealth, happiness and prosperity. Presented as a one-page look at your complete financial picture, it illuminates strengths, reveals weaknesses, and delivers options by providing a list of direct actions to accomplish. Fundamentally, it examines and illustrates a total process for the engineering of your dreams. This blueprint also provides mathematical calculations verifying that there is a more efficient way to accelerate your wealth. These strategies are designed to create better benefits, greater money supply, and improved cash flow to enhance your lifestyle without spending any more than you are currently spending today.

Who do you think are the happiest in retirement: the ones who are chasing the market or the ones who have a guaranteed monthly and annual income each year? The majority of people I know do not like to chase inconsistency or volatility of the market; they love certainty. Did you know that anxiety is created by uncertainty? Who wants visions of their retirement to be consumed by severe anxiety? No one I can think of, and that's the last thing I'd want for anyone, especially my clients.

Retirement should be a time in people's lives to enjoy and take advantage of certain freedoms, especially with their time, which most people have to sacrifice during their working years to earn a living. However, many Americans will be faced with a sharp decrease in their income when they retire. I have never met anyone who wants to reduce their income when they retire. They want to live the "golden life" in retirement; the life they were always promised. So many people have not saved or planned appropriately throughout their working years. They may have lived a wonderful lifestyle, lived life to the fullest and took care of their responsibilities, but now when the day comes and sacrifices must be made, reality sets in.

Some baby boomers will still have pensions, and many have saved in their 401(k) or 403(b), which is great. But the fundamental question and analysis that needs to take place is, "Will it be enough to generate the same amount of income I was making while working, and enable me to live on it for the rest of my life, into my 90's or beyond, for my retirement?" That is the crucial question and the reason why the number one fear on people's minds today is the fear of running out of money. Regrettably, for many people, this fear is well founded, and the consequences of countless personal fiscal shortfalls will sadly transpire over the coming years. Believe me, following the cyclical nature of the market, people will run out of money based on market volatility, by taking too high of an annual distribution, as well as the extensive costs and expenses that the average consumer is exposed to today.

Are you worried that this will be you? What if you could attain the security of knowing that such devastation cannot happen to you, regardless of what happens to the markets? This is the security I specialize in creating, through income distribution planning. Along with protecting your human life value, you can establish a permission slip to act as asset protection and ensure your legacy is always there for your loved ones and estate.

Today, the Prudent Investor Rule limits the amount fiduciaries should distribute from a client's assets in retirement. The 4% rule used to be the standard that determined the income needed to sustain individuals in retirement; however, that rule was conceived in the nineties and things have changed. Today, amid the low interest rate environment and longer life expectancies, in combination with the volatility of the market, many in the financial planning industry have reduced the recommended distribution amount.[7]

Let's consider an example. Suppose you have $1 million in an account, from which you can take out $21,800 out per year to sustain your life through your life expectancy. Does that make you feel like a millionaire today? My guess would be, probably not.

Now, let's assume your annual household income before retirement was $175,000. To determine your retirement income, we'll use values based on an average American household.

> $36,000 – Social Security, Husband (at 67)
> $18,000 – Social Security, Wife
> <u>$21,800 </u>– Interest Distributions from 401(k)
> $75,800 – Total Annual Income

So, let's think about this for a moment. Even after successfully accumulating $1 million in a qualified retirement account, you are looking at an annual retirement income that is 56.7% less than when you were working. With this in mind, does it come as a surprise that so many people say they can't stop working?

Another concern is that the majority of workers today no longer have pensions to help overcome such an income drop. Even more alarming is the outlook for future generations who will not have pensions and face an unclear future for Social Security. Despite only having their 401(k) accounts to support their retirement, most people are only saving a fraction of what they need to, with two-thirds of all Americans failing to contribute to a retirement plan at all[8].

We have a crisis in the distribution and protection phase of retirement planning throughout our country today. People need real help, and many are at a loss for where to turn. Can you afford to live off of 56.7% less then what you are earning today? In the previous example, that equates living on $99,200 less of income, *every single year* for the rest of your life.

Now, let's reimagine a similar example for our clients, Mr. and Mrs. Wealth By Design, only with a few adjustments. Let's suppose they own $2 million of permanent whole life insurance which creates a "permission slip" to spend down more of their assets while they are living. This

employs life insurance as more than just a
death benefit when one person passes away.

> $36,000 – Social Security, Husband (at 67)
> $18,000 – Social Security, Wife
> $65,000 – Spend Down of 401k Principle &
>   Interest at 4%
> <u>$60,000</u> – Spend Down of Life Ins. Cash Value
> $179,000 – Total Annual Income

In this case, the clients can spend down their
401(k) savings over their lifetime because of the
financial safety net the permanent life
insurance will provide upon either spouse's
passing. In addition, the permanent life
insurance provides a cash value which the
clients can spend down, tax-free, when
designed properly. Overall, with a total annual
income of $179,000, this example provides a
stark contrast to the previous one, not only
preventing a devastating drop in income at
retirement, but actually increasing the retirees'
annual income compared to when they were
working.

The important point here is, even if Mr. Wealth
By Design passes away during this retirement
phase of life, there is a residual death benefit for

Mrs. Wealth By Design which will continue to provide tax-free income for the rest of her life.

The difference between these two examples exhibits the leverage of thoughtful planning and provides an illustration of how powerful a tool insurance can be. We are merely scratching the surface of the extent to which your *Action Blueprint* can illuminate the key areas of focus and crucial steps required to achieve a dramatic impact on your journey to an ideal and secure future.

Chapter 11

Acceleration In Action

With all of the preparation completed, we are here as you begin implementing your *Wealth Acceleration Plan* and making things happen. This is a very exciting time because all your efforts are coming to fruition and now you get to see the results of your *Action Blueprint*.

Bob MacDonald says, "Success comes down to doing simple things and simply doing them." This is the time for you to act upon the plan that has been laid out for you and, indeed, begin to witness the profound difference you are capable of making in your life and for your future.

So much has happened building up to this point. You have dedicated your time and efforts to allow me to help you on one of the most crucial aspects in determining the path your future will take. Together we have gone through the discovery and review, your present situation, as well as strategies to implement to launch your dream financial world into action. Take a moment to reflect. How does this feel? How do you feel? This has been a complete transformation from the person you were before and how you thought. Now the acceleration for your financial success begins. The implementation of all of your decisions begins: your action plan.

Where do you want your financial future to lead?

It's all up to you.

I act as a guide to help you navigate as efficiently and mindfully as possible. There is no one particular product that does anything magical on its own. Effective planning is all about how you strategically orchestrate everything to work together. There is, however, a mathematical science behind every recommendation and no individual, couple, family or business is ever the same. Thus, every recommendation I make or strategy you employ is completely unique. As you can see, your wealth is by design. I do my very best to make the planning process highly logical and protect you, your loved ones and your estate over time, into longevity. Now it is your turn to take action and accomplish real progress in the acceleration phase.

One of my favorite quotes is by Vince Lombardi. "Perfection is not attainable, but if we chase perfection we can catch excellence." Not one of us will ever be perfect, but we can, and certainly should, pursue excellence throughout our lives.

Chapter 12

Accountability Factor

Without a substantial element of accountability, even the greatest intentions and most carefully made plans are far less likely to be effectively brought to fruition. I am here to support you on your path to success, and the last thing I want to see happen is for all of the time, energy, and effort you've invested into changing the direction of your financial future to go to waste. To ensure you stay on track, I arrange a private coaching session as well as monthly, quarterly and annual review meetings. This is another way in which I set myself apart and raise the expectations for my clients beyond that of other financial professionals.

So, I ask you, are you ready to take action? Are you ready to take massive action to get your life back and on the right track? You only have one life, and your future is entirely up to you!

You may think with all of the research and information available today you can take a do-it-yourself approach, but I ask you: How is it going for you? Are you asking all the right questions? Do you know all the right questions to ask? Will you be ok, financially, if you experience a health event? What does the survivor income look like for your spouse, at various ages? There are so many more questions to ask and the list goes on.

When the market is doing great, you may be feeling alright; but when the market corrects, you could be left feeling as though you have no idea what just happened, or what to do next. In reality, the majority of people only have access to the limited information that is offered to consumers. Do you have the means to obtain information that is published for professionals? Perhaps you do but, my guess is, probably not.

Please don't think that I am minimizing what you have accomplished. You are doing the very best you can, with the information you have at your disposal. However, there is a professional for everything and, in every profession, there are good and bad professionals within the industry. There is a reason that you are reading this book. You are questioning the knowledge that's available at your fingertips. You are questioning the information that has been offered to you by your current broker or advisor.

I would venture to guess that the material here has been presented to you for the first time and your current broker or advisor has never said any of this to you before. Why? They want you to continue trying to accumulate your assets and keep your money in the market so they can continue making money, whether you do or not. Ultimately, it doesn't matter to them whether you are making money and paying an enormous amount of fees and expenses. Even if you are in a down or depressed market, you are still stuck paying fees and expenses that benefit their bottom line. How is that fair? Quite frankly, it's not. I don't believe it's right and I don't want you to do it anymore; that is why I had to start talking about this and stand up for people like you.

So, are you ready make a change? You have to take action, massive action, but I am here to support you all along the way. I will educate you and start you in the right direction. It's not necessarily about trying to get ahead in the traditional way; it's about getting ahead by being educated the right way.

You were always told to pay yourself before you paid everyone else. Don't let everyone else take from your profits before you get paid. In today's age, the government is the first one with their hand out to get paid with your paycheck. Choose to become educated. You deserve better, and you know you do, so stop the madness. Reflect upon all of the money you have worked so hard for, on top of all the sacrifices that you have made over your lifetime. Consider the time spent away from your spouses, your children and extended family. Truly; stop and think. You deserve this! What do you actually want? Now? One year from now? Three years from now? Five years from now? Ten years from now? What do you envision for your legacy, honestly? Achieving your destiny is all up to you and it is, in fact, time to take massive action to accomplish your true purpose. Now, are you ready or do you just want to talk about it?

References

1 – The Federal Reserve. "Consumer Credit Outstanding Table, 2017." January 8, 2018. www.federalreserve.gov/releases/g19/current/default.htm

2 – Social Security Administration. "Period Life Table, 2014" Actuarial Life Table. December 12, 2017. www.ssa.gov/OACT/STATS/table4c6.html

3 – Sullivan, Missy. "Lost Inheritance." The Wall Street Journal Online. March 8, 2013. www.wsj.com/articles/SB10001424127887324662404578334663271139552

4 – Dickler, Jessica. "How Long $1 Million Will Last in Retirement." CNBC, August 21, 2017. www.cnbc.com/2017/08/21/how-long-1-million-will-last-in-retirement.html

5 – Social Security Administration. Calculators: Life Expectancy. December 18, 2017. www.ssa.gov/planners/lifeexpectancy.html

6 – Dickler, Jessica. "How to Prepare for Being 'Suddenly Single'" CNBC, September 5, 2017. www.cnbc.com/2017/09/05/how-to-prepare-for-being-suddenly-single.html

7 – Frankel, Matthew. "4 Serious Problems With the 4% Retirement Rule" The Motley Fool Online, Septemeber 10, 2017. www.fool.com/retirement/2017/09/10/4-serious-problems-with-the-4-retirement-rule.aspx

8 – Bhattarai, Abha. "Two-Thirds of Americans Aren't Using This Easy Way to Save for Retirement" The Washington Post, February 22,2017. www.washingtonpost.com/news/get-there/wp/2017/02/22/two-in-three-americans-will-never-retire-at-this-rate/?utm_term=.14f4c44c9164

About the Author

Elisabeth Dawson, RFC, LUTCF
President and CEO
Copia Wealth Management
& Insurance Services

Elisabeth Dawson is the founder of Copia Wealth Management & Insurance Services, an organization that provides financial and insurance advising with education to help her clients achieve their desired wealth goals. Her organization's macroeconomic approach begins with a comprehensive evaluation of a client's "wish list" and financial engineering strategies to achieve successful results with minimized risk. Unlike other traditional financial planning firms, Copia Wealth Management & Insurance Services educates and counsels clients through every financial task and decision in their lives.

Elisabeth specializes in working with entrepreneurs, small businesses, individuals, couples, families and multi-generational legacy families. Her financial areas of expertise include: insurance, various investment strategies, income protection, tax mitigation strategies, and wealth accumulation strategies. With 19 years of experience, Elisabeth is more passionate than ever about helping as many people as possible to achieve the dream of their own ideal future and exceed their expectations for a secure retirement.